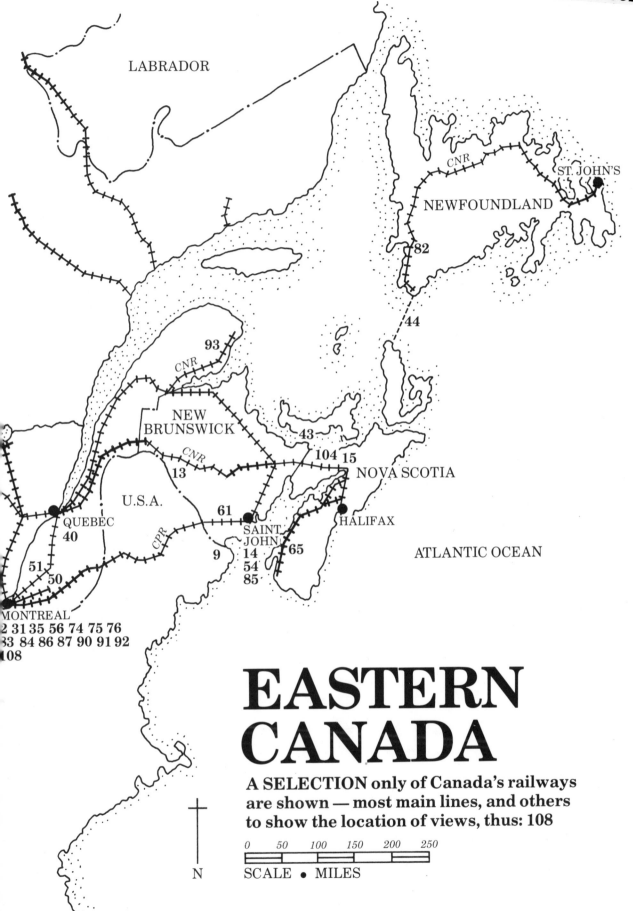

LABRADOR

CNR

ST. JOHN'S

NEWFOUNDLAND

82

44

93

CNR

NEW
BRUNSWICK

43

104 15

CNR

13

NOVA SCOTIA

U.S.A.

61

HALIFAX

QUEBEC

SAINT
JOHN

ATLANTIC OCEAN

40

CPR

9

14
54
85

65

51

50

MONTREAL
2 31 35 56 74 75 76
33 84 86 87 90 91 92
108

EASTERN
CANADA

A SELECTION only of Canada's railways
are shown — most main lines, and others
to show the location of views, thus: 108

0   50   100   150   200   250

N

SCALE • MILES

CANADIAN RAILWAYS
IN PICTURES

1 *Tubular Bridge at St. Henry's Falls*, oil painting on canvas by Cornelius Krieghoff (1815-1872), often called "Canada's national artist." The bridge spanning the St. Henry's Falls on the Etchemin River, four miles west of Levis, was built in 1854 by the Quebec and Richmond Railway, a line taken over by the Grand Trunk Railway and later incorporated in the Intercolonial Railway from Halifax to Montreal. The bridge shown was used until 1900.

Reproduction, McCord Museum, McGill University, Montreal; thanks to R.H. Hubbard and A.N. Wainwright, Jr.

ROBERT F. LEGGET

CANADIAN RAILWAYS
IN PICTURES

Douglas & McIntyre
Vancouver/Toronto

Douglas & McIntyre
1615 Venables Street
Vancouver, British Columbia
V5L 2H1

Canadian Cataloguing in Publication Data

Legget, Robert F., 1904-
    Canadian railways in pictures

    ISBN 0-88914-052-9 (bound)
    ISBN 0-88894-423-3 (pbk)
    1. Railroads—Canada—Pictorial works.
I. Title.
TF26.L433   385′.0971   C77-002176-X

Typesetting by Domino-Link Ltd.
Cover design by Barbara Hodgson
Cover image courtesy of Canadian
    Pacific Archives — *Travel Canadian
    Across Canada!* (c. 1940's)
Book design by Nancy Legue
Printed and bound in Hong Kong

Contents

Acknowledgments

THE ORIGINAL IDEA for this book arose because of the difficulties encountered in selecting a small number of illustrations for *Railroads of Canada*. I am therefore indebted to Mr. T. Stanhope Sprigg for this initial suggestion and to Mr. David St. John Thomas for his valued encouragement. Once again I am indebted to Mr. S.S. Worthen, editor of *Canadian Rail* of Montreal, for his interest and sage counsel. Satisfactory features of the book will often be due to him; its many imperfections are my responsibility.

On this page are listed the sources of many photographs. I am grateful for being able to include them in this volume. It will thus be seen that I am again indebted to the photographic archives of Canadian Pacific, Canadian National Railways and the British Columbia Railways; and so to Messrs. O.S.A. Lavallée and D. Jones (CPR); Miss S. Gallagher (CNR), and Mr. H.D. Armstrong (BCR).

For older photographs, I have been privileged to sample some of the fine archival records that Canada possesses. The Public Archives of Canada (Dr. W. Smith, Dominion Archivist) and members of the Picture Division too numerous to mention individually; Mr. L.K. Ingersoll, then director of the New Brunswick Museum and members of his staff; Miss M. Van Every of the Ontario Archives; Mrs. E. Kreisel of the Alberta Archives; Mrs. G. Barrass (and earlier Mrs. S. Baptie) of the Glenbow Foundation, Calgary; Mr. H. Gulliver of Victoria, in procuring views from the British Columbia Archives; and Mr. S. Triggs of the Notman Photographic Archives, McGill University—all have been most helpful.

From across the border I have received friendly aid from Father E.J. Dowling, S.J. and Mr. E. Treloar. Reverend J. Allen Gibson of Chester, N.S., Mr. D. Hoskins of Coppercliff, and Dr. R.K. Ryan of Toronto kindly provided special photographs which unfortunately could not be used. And Mr. O.R. Woermke of Thurso, Que., loaned me the photograph from which plate 63 was prepared.

So diverse and widespread are the railways of Canada serving this vast land, and so interesting are their varied histories that, within the confines of a slim book such as this, only glimpses can be presented of their development. It is hoped that the selection of pictures will give at least some idea of their fascination even today.

Robert F. Legget   *Ottawa, Canada*

Sources of Photographs

Alberta Archives, Ernest Brown Collection: 18, 20, 21, 25, 30, 32, 59

Archives of Ontario: 6, 12, 67, 68

Canadian National Railways: 42, 43, 44, 50, 51, 52, 57, 76, 87, 92, 108, 113

Editor, *Canadian Rail*: 40

Canadian Pacific Archives: 7, 35, 37, 46, 47, 86, 89, 107, 116

Canadian Railroad Historical Association Archives, E.A. Toohey Collection: 95

Detroit Maritime Historical Museum, Father E.J. Dowling, S.J., Curator: 39

The Glenbow Foundation, Calgary: 16, 17, 23, 26, 27, 28, 29, 60

Gaetan Lafleur, Thurso: 63

Mrs. Stuart M. Lawson, Toronto: 3

R.F. Legget: 34, 36, 38, 41, 56, 58, 62, 64, 65, 74, 75, 79, 80, 81, 82, 83, 84, 85, 90, 91, 93, 94, 101, 102, 103, 105, 109, 110, 111, 112, 114, 115, 118

National Film Board of Canada: 88

New Brunswick Museum; C.W. Anderson Collection: 2. Original print from collection of the late John Loye

New Brunswick Museum: 4

New Brunswick Museum, C.W. Anderson Collection: 9, 10, 14, 15, 54, 61

New Brunswick Museum, C.L. Brown Collection: 11, 13

The Notman Photographic Archives, McCord Museum, McGill University, Montreal: 31

Provincial Archives of British Columbia: 19, 45

Public Archives of Canada: 5, 8, 22, 24, 33, 48, 49, 55, 66, 69, 70, 71, 72, 73, 106

Railfare Enterprises Ltd., Montreal: 96, 97, 98, 99, 100; Patterson-George, Brown and Rossiter collections

Photograph by Ken Talbot; courtesy of British Columbia Railway: 78

Elmer Treloar, Highland Park, Michigan: 77, 104

Introduction

THE RAILWAYS OF CANADA today span the country from Atlantic to Pacific, from the U.S. border to the Arctic and the shores of Hudson Bay. Almost all of the more than 40,000 miles of operating lines are single track, because of the limited traffic, but the double-track Montreal-Toronto-Sarnia line, leading to Chicago, is one of the great "main lines" of North America. The nation-wide system is operated by about two dozen companies, Canadian Pacific accounting for about one third of the total and Canadian National Railways for just over one half. Total mileage has not changed significantly in the last 40 years, new lines replacing those abandoned, but from 1870 to 1920, after a slow start following 1836, there was steady extension of railways across the land. Building of the CPR to the west coast was but a part of this; construction of the Intercolonial (now CNR) from Halifax to Montreal preceded the CPR by more than ten years. This book presents a sampling of the photographic record so fortunately available of this great story.

The Beginnings

CANADA'S FIRST RAILWAY—the first train ran 21 July 1836—was between La Prairie, on the mainland south of Montreal Island, and St. Jean on the Richelieu River. It was followed by a few other short portage railways in the Province of Canada and by some small mine railways in the Maritime Provinces. Only 68 miles were in operation by 1850, but "railway fever" then gripped Canada, a crucial development being the start of the Grand Trunk Railway in 1852. Montreal and Toronto were linked in 1856. Official adoption of a 5ft 6in gauge in 1851 interfered with progress, but standard gauge was accepted in the 1870s. By this time, railway construction had started in the west. Photography in its earliest simple forms was contemporaneous with these developments.

2

3 *The first Toronto Railway Station of the Grand Trunk Railway, in 1857, as seen in a copy of a painting by William Armstrong (1822-1914), an engineer, artist and early photographer who thus recorded many early events in what is now Ontario. The original has been lost. (Reproduced from a copy courtesy of Mrs. Stuart Lawson, Toronto.)*

4 *Canada's oldest existing locomotive, the* Samson, *built in Newcastle-on-Tyne by Timothy Hackworth in 1838, and now on permanent display in the centre of New Glasgow, Nova Scotia, near to which it worked on a mine railway to Pictou Wharf. It was fired from the front but is here shown coupled to the oldest Canadian railway coach. After being built in England and shipped to Halifax, Nova Scotia, in 1838, it was first used by the new governor and his bride. The "Bride's Coach" is now on display at the Baltimore and Ohio RR Transportation Museum, Baltimore, Maryland, U.S.A.*

5 *The Carillon and Grenville Railway's Portage Train which ran the twelve miles between Carillon and Grenville on the Ottawa River from 1854 to 1910 during summer months, linking the steamship services on two portions of the river separated by great rapids, and paralleling the small canals that circumvented these. Built to the "provincial gauge" of 5ft 6in, it had the distinction of being the last remaining broad-gauge railway in North America, never being converted to standard gauge. Supplies of wood for use as fuel can be seen.*

6 *Paris Junction in southwestern Ontario in 1860, showing a diamond crossing of broad gauge lines on the Great Western Railway (of Canada). GWR converted all its lines to standard gauge between 1870 and 1873, and was taken over by the Grand Trunk in 1882.*

7 *The first locomotive in the prairies, a small construction locomotive, being unloaded off a barge at St. Boniface, Manitoba, in 1877 after being brought by water from Fargo, North Dakota. Built by Baldwin's in Philadelphia in 1870, it was later named the* Countess of Dufferin *and is now on view in Winnipeg after a varied career.*

Early Days in Eastern Canada

COMPLETION OF THE MONTREAL to Toronto line by the Grand Trunk with its connection to Chicago through Sarnia was only one, although the principal, of the lines built between 1850 and 1860 in what is now Ontario. Lines were built running north from small ports on Lake Ontario, mainly for lumber shipment. Rail connections were forged between Niagara Falls and Lake Huron, at Goderich, between Toronto-Hamilton and Windsor-Detroit. In what is now Quebec, Montreal was linked with Quebec City and Rivière du Loup, and with the Atlantic at Portland, Maine. Small lines were also built in the Maritime Provinces. Their construction led to the great concept of a rail link with Montreal, which was completed in 1876 and named the Intercolonial Railway. Simple as they were, these early lines transformed life patterns in eastern Canada.

8

8 *The start of new railway construction was cause for public celebration in those days, as shown by this William Armstrong painting which depicts the turning of the first sod for the Toronto, Grey and Bruce Railway. HRH Prince Arthur officiated on 5 October 1869 at Weston, near Toronto.*

9 *The St. Stephen Railway of New Brunswick, later to become part of the CPR, was one of the early local Maritime lines; this view (1866) of the first locomotive of the line, with the roofs of St. Stephen in the background, demonstrates local pride in this new facility.*

9

10 *Originally built to narrow gauge, the New Brunswick Railway was a rather more important Maritime line in the early days before it became part of the CPR. Its locomotives were built in the U.S.A. This view shows delivery arrangements for an early machine.*

11 *A later locomotive of the New Brunswick Railway was No. 9, built in Kingston, Canada, in 1866 for the Nova Scotia Railway. After its New Brunswick service it became No. 488 of the CPR, remaining in active use until being scrapped in 1895.*

10

11

12 *Canada's Great Western Railway Company served well that part of southwestern Ontario between Hamilton, Niagara Falls and Windsor, providing an international connection between "The Falls" and Windsor-Detroit. This typical example of their locomotive stud is* *typical also of the locomotives of other early Ontario lines. The* Adam Brown *hauled the first GWR train into Elora on 1 July 1870.*

12

13 *Although their safety record is generally good, accidents have happened on Canadian railways. This scene at Grand Falls, New Brunswick, shows what resulted when a local CPR train failed to cross the Saint John River on 22 June 1900. The locomotive, No. 508, was submerged, but the train crew and the single passenger in the one coach all escaped.*

13

14 *One of the famous bridges of eastern Canada is that over the Reversing Falls at the mouth of the Saint John River, New Brunswick, in the city of Saint John. Here is the first bridge at this historic and scenic site. It was erected in 1885, and served until it was replaced by a modern steel bridge in 1913.*

14

15 *The Intercolonial Railway from Halifax to Montreal was opened for service on 1 July 1876; its construction was an epic story, second only to the building of the CPR a decade later. It still serves as the CNR main line from Montreal to Halifax, and its general appearance differs little from this view taken in 1901 in the Wentworth Valley, Nova Scotia. The* Maritime Express *is hauled by ICR No. 69, built by the Manchester Locomotive Works in 1901; it eventually became CNR No. 1522.*

15

16 *The last rail of the CPR was laid at 9:22 a.m. on 7 November 1885 at Craigellachie British Columbia. Donald Smith, later Lord Strathcona, hammered in the ceremonial last spike that afternoon and the event was recorded in one of the most famous of all railway photographs. This less familar view is a record of another "last spike" that was driven on the same day at Golden, B.C. A member of the Royal Northwest Mounted Police (in his pillbox hat) was apparently the only official observer of this event.*

Building the Canadian Pacific

THE WELL KNOWN STORY of the building of the Canadian Pacific Railway between 1881 and 1886, still one of the epics of railway construction, was but the culmination of work which started in 1872. Part of the agreement which brought British Columbia into Confederation was an undertaking by the government of Canada to complete construction of a railway linking the new province with eastern Canada within ten years from the date of union. Sandford Fleming, although still busy as chief engineer for the building of the Intercolonial Railway, was called upon to organize the necessary survey work, starting in the summer of 1872 with a personal tour of inspection across the country to the Pacific coast. Forty-six thousand miles of lines were studied on foot, 11,500 miles being actually surveyed. As many as 2,000 men were engaged on this task, in its way as great an achievement as the final construction. Construction also started under Fleming, 700 miles being completed by government forces to be passed over to CPR when the final stage commenced.

16

17 *Prior to completion of the CPR, freight had to be taken through the mountains of the west by pack train. Here is Don Mann's pack train working its way through the rugged terrain near Golden, B.C., on a trail immediately above rock excavation for the railway right-of-way.*

18 *Some idea of the terrain is given by this view of completed track in the vicinity of Mount Carroll. Protection against snow avalanches had already been found necessary.*

19 *Construction of the transcontinental railway by the government of Canada started on the Pacific Coast as well as on the prairies, and in British Columbia, Andrew Onderdonk was responsible for the first contract work. This early view shows construction approaching the Coast Range Mountains.*

20 *Man-power was responsible for most of the work of construction, but animals were also used when possible. Here, timber piles which have been cut from the forests for bridge supports are being driven by real horse-power.*

21 *The first bridge across Stoney Creek on the long climb up to Roger's Pass through which the new line was able to penetrate the Selkirk Range of mountains. The modern bridge replacing this early structure will be seen on page 45.*

21

22 *Once the first river crossings had been constructed, they had to be protected against scour around bridge piers. This is an early work train on the CPR dumping protective rock-fill at Revelstoke, British Columbia.*

23 *The building of the Canadian Pacific Railway was directed by the genius of William Cornelius Van Horne (later to be Sir William). Here is a rare glimpse of the great general manager at Stoney Creek, B.C. on one of his inspection trips, surrounded by a group of his associates and assistants; Sir Casimir Gzowski is on the extreme right.*

24 *Quite the most remarkable railway in Canada, still, is the 110-mile-long White Pass and Yukon Route, which links Skagway in Alaska on the coast with Whitehorse, capital city of the Yukon Territory. In its first 20 miles it rises almost 3,000 feet; grades can be imagined. This view will aid imagination, since it shows excavation proceeding near the summit of the Pass and some of the 35,000 men who worked on this unique enterprise.*

23

Other Western Railroad Building

FOR ALMOST TWENTY YEARS the CPR was the only line linking eastern Canada with British Columbia. In the closing years of the century, heroic effort created the isolated narrow-gauge White Pass and Yukon line to give access to the Klondike country, but it was not until the start of the twentieth century that the transcontinental monopoly of the CPR was challenged. Two more transcontinental railways were then built, the Canadian Northern and the Grand Trunk Pacific. Both followed a route to the north of the Canadian Pacific by making use of the Yellowhead Pass, Sandford Fleming's own choice for the original Canadian Pacific location. The Canadian Northern then turned south to reach the coast at Vancouver while the Grand Trunk Pacific turned north to the new port, named Prince Rupert, that was established five hundred miles north of Vancouver. Both lines are now part of Canadian National Railways; their construction provides two more vivid chapters in the history of Canadian railway building.

24

25 *Grading on the Grand Trunk Pacific in prairie country near Clover Bar with a fourteen-horse elevating grader, perhaps the ultimate development of horse-operated mobile equipment. Eight horses pulled the grader; six pushed it through a cross bar arrangement. Soil was raised and dumped into carts which could come and go from beneath the dumping chute.*

25

COPYRIGHT
PHOTO BY
ERNEST BROWN
341 A

GRADING ON
G.T.P. AT
CLOVER BAR
SHOWING 16 HORSE
PLOW AT WORK

26 *The Frontier College of Canada provides educational and recreational services to construction men and others working in isolation from normal settlement. Devoted staff of the college did yeoman work during the great years of railway building in the west. Here is one of their reading tents at a construction camp for the Canadian Northern Railway, in 1911.*

26

27 *First expansion of the Canadian Northern Railway from its small beginnings near Winnipeg was across the prairies. This is the first train to enter young Fort Saskatchewan, just to the east of Edmonton. The date was 8 November 1905.*

27

28 *Arrival of steel 16 days later at Edmonton, then at the start of its development as the capital city of Alberta, was rather more elaborate. This is the crowd which gathered for the ceremonial driving of the last spike on 24 November 1905.*

28

29 *Mechanical equipment was now supplementing manpower in railway building. This mechanical track-laying machine was in use on the Grand Trunk Pacific Railway as early as 1909 near Wainwright, Alberta.*

30 *Completion of the second transcontinental line, the Grand Trunk Pacific, was overshadowed by the outbreak of World War I, but this a photographic record was made of the final linking up of steel early in 1914.*

29

30

Winter Conditions

RUDYARD KIPLING IGNORED three seasons when he dubbed Canada "Our Lady of the Snows," but it is true that snow and ice give railwaymen problems in winter. The snow and ice that accumulate on rolling stock in bad winter storms go far to explain the necessarily heavy appearance of Canadian trains. Snow clearing from tracks has been developed into a real art and is now accomplished by sophisticated modern equipment. Avalanche warning systems in the mountains now supplement the safeguards provided by snow-sheds. Only rarely is rail traffic actually stopped by winter conditions. In the very early years, advantage was taken of winter ice covers on rivers to use these as natural bridges.

31 *The Montreal Ice Railway, here photographed in action by one of Canada's early master photographers, linked two lines instead of vessels used to transport railway equipment while the St. Lawrence River was open. Rails were laid on timbers arranged in cribs on the river ice. Starting in 1880, small trains were operated from 30 January 1880 until the end of March and similarly for three winters thereafter.*

32,33 *Snowplough operation is always spectacular as well as hazardous. These two views from early in the century are typical of operations of the rotary plough, a Canadian invention.*

32

33

34 *Even with modern equipment and advanced methods of snow control, handwork is still necessary on occasion, as shown by this view of switch-cleaning at Field, British Columbia, of a westbound CPR transcontinental train.*

34

35 *What can happen! A main-line diesel locomotive at Windsor Station, Montreal, CPR, after arrival from a night run through a bad blizzard.*

Railways and Waterways

CANADA'S FIRST RAILWAYS were essentially improvements to existing portage trails and roads around rapids (such as the Carillon Portage Railway, p. 12), or to roads providing short-cuts between rivers (such as the La Prairie to St. Jean line, pp. 8 and 52). The close links between railways in Canada and the country's waterways remain, even though many of the pleasant combined rail and water journeys have now disappeared with the decline in passenger rail patronage. Train ferries still connect the mainland with principal islands, such as Prince Edward Island, but as well as freight cars they now carry automobiles instead of sleeping cars. Over-water transport of railway equipment is yet another little-known chapter in the record of Canadian railroading, one essential to the national transportation service that the railways still provide.

36 *One of the most famous of the combined rail-water journeys was that provided for many years by CPR from Toronto to the head of the Great Lakes. Passengers went by special train from Toronto's Union Station to Port McNicoll on Georgian Bay, Lake Huron, there boarding a splendidly equipped lake vessel for Port Arthur/ Fort William (now Thunder Bay). One of these vessels is here seen in the 1950s at the Port McNicoll wharf together with its service train.*

37 *Most isolated of all the portage railways was the Atlin Short Line and Navigation Company's line, known as the Atlin Tramway,* opened on 6 June 1899. Only two and a half miles long, it connected Scotia Bay on Atlin Lake with Taku Arm in far northern British Columbia. Down Taku Arm, connection could be made with navigation on the Yukon River and so with the Klondike, the Tramway being another development linked with the gold mining in that region at the turn of the century.

38 *The little Duchess is now on display at Carcross on the White Pass line, together with other reminders of the travel facilities of the early days.*

37

39 *One of the important car-ferry services
linking Canadian and U.S. rail systems was
that across the Detroit River at Windsor-Detroit
connecting CNR with lines of its U.S.
subsidiary, the Grand Trunk Western Railroad.
One of the famous vessels of this service was the
iron-hulled* Lansdowne, *here seen bucking the
ice during a difficult winter crossing. Built in
Michigan in 1884, she could carry 16 freight
cars on two tracks.*

39

40 *One of the most unusual railway ferries ever to operate on Canadian waters was the SS* Leonard, *here seen on her speed trials. Built in England by Cammell Laird and Co., she served for three vital years (1915-18) to link two sections of the then-new National Transcontinental Railway across the St. Lawrence River until the Quebec Bridge was ready for use. The unusual deck was moveable to allow loading whatever the river level, which changed with local tidal conditions.*

40

41 *One of the most remarkable rail-water services has been that supplying the western Arctic with its freight. After being brought north from Edmonton on Northern Alberta Railways, for about thirty years freight was trans-shipped at Waterways onto barges of the Hudson's Bay Company and the Northern Transportation Company. Stern-wheeler steamboats or diesel tugs pushed the barges to Fort Fitzgerald, whence freight was portaged for 12 miles and again loaded on barges for the final 1,200-mile sail down the Mackenzie River system to the Arctic coast. This shows the trans-shipping wharf at Waterways, NAR freight cars in the background. The service is now operated from Hay River on Great Slave Lake* *(see p. 96)*.

41

42 *Rail freight connections between the mainland of British Columbia and Vancouver Island have been effected by an extensive system of tugs and rail-equipped barges. Fine fleets of passenger vessels have supplemented this simple freight service in the protected waters of the Inside Passage. The service has now been extended from Prince Rupert up the coast, still in protected waters, to serve isolated Alaskan ports, at one of which CNR cars are loaded with pulp and paper products for barging to railhead at Prince Rupert. Equipment is even barged in this way for delivery to the Alaskan Railroad at Anchorage.*

42

43,44 *On Canada's east coast, with no protected waterway, fully equipped ocean-going vessels are needed for car ferry services to Prince Edward Island and Newfoundland. Two of the most modern vessels are here shown: the* Abegweit, *which serves The Island (P.E.I.), and the* Leif Ericson, *which serves Newfoundland from North Sydney in Cape Breton. There is overnight accommodation for passengers on the long Newfoundland passage. Both vessels are equipped with multiple rail tracks; cars to Newfoundland have to be transferred at Port-aux-Basques to narrow-gauge tracks for operation on the narrow-gauge system of the former Newfoundland Railway.*

43

44

Bridges and Tunnels

THE SIZE OF CANADA'S RIVERS has necessitated many great bridges and innumerable small ones for the linking of rail lines. The Victoria Bridge, 9,144ft long between abutments, was opened as early as 1860 to link the city and island of Montreal with the mainland to the south, and is still one of the great bridges of the world. So also is the Quebec Bridge with its record-breaking cantilever span. These are but two of many. The Dunblane Bridge across the South Saskatchewan River is over one thousand miles from the sea and yet is 1,771ft long between abutments. Bridge construction has, therefore, been a vital part of the development of Canada's railway system. Tunnels, on the other hand, are infrequent on Canadian lines. There are some of importance in cities; the Spiral Tunnels and the Connaught tunnel in the mountains of the west were improvements to the CPR main line; the St. Clair Tunnel is unique in being an international link.

45 *The uses of timber are well shown by this Niagara Canyon trestle bridge on the Esquimalt and Nanaimo Railway (now part of the CPR) on Vancouver Island. This was typical of the remarkable bridges in rough country built with rare woodsman's skill from timbers obtained nearby. Most of these great timber trestles have now been replaced by more modern structures.*

45

46 *In great contrast is the steel Lethbridge Viaduct (Canadian Pacific) built in 1909, the longest and highest trestle bridge in Canada and perhaps in North America. It is 5,328ft long and 314ft high above the Oldman River of Alberta.*

47 *Another notable CPR bridge is the modern Stoney Creek Bridge (replacing that seen on p. 24). Built in 1893 as a 336ft three-hinged steel arch, this fine structure was reinforced in 1929 for heavier traffic. A most ingenious piece of daring structural engineering permitted the reinforcement work to go on without disrupting normal traffic.*

47

48,49 *In order to obtain a through connection with Chicago and U.S. rail lines to the west, the Grand Trunk Railway decided to replace car ferries across the St. Clair River, between Sarnia and Port Huron, with an underwater tunnel. Begun in 1889 and officially opened on 19 September 1891, it was one of the pioneer river crossings by tunnel. Trains were at first hauled through by a special stud of powerful 0-10-0 Baldwin locomotives. Electrical traction was adopted in 1906, making this short electric railway through the tunnel another pioneer venture.*

50 *Level crossings constitute a special problem for the very long railways of Canada which intersect with many roads. Limited traffic on many lines obviates the replacement of crossings by costly bridges. Good progress is being made, however, in all settled parts of the country. This pleasing rigid-frame reinforced* *concrete bridge of CNR at St. Hilaire, Quebec, demonstrates the attention being paid to aesthetics.*

50

51 *Even with the best attention to maintenance, bridge piers sometimes have to be replaced. To do this without interfering with normal traffic involves civil engineering design and construction of a high order. This view shows how the main CNR line from Montreal to the East was maintained while a bridge pier in the Richelieu River was removed, prior to replacement, at Beloeil. Steel bearing piles have been driven within the steel pile cofferdam in which the new pier will be built.*

52 *Another procedure for smaller bridges, pioneered by Canadian railway engineers, has been the building of complete reinforced concrete bridge slabs, finished off with rail fastenings and all other necessary fittings, on special supports adjacent to the bridge span that has to be replaced. Usually on Sunday mornings, access to the track is given for a few hours and breakdown cranes are used to remove the old span and to place the new span in position. This is a relatively small example of such a slab being placed on the CNR line at Aurora, north of Toronto.*

52

53 *When the Shand Dam of the Grand River Conservation Authority in southwestern Ontario was constructed in 1939, a small branch line of CPR serving the town of Fergus had to be displaced. Instead of building a new bridge or engaging in an elaborate relocation, engineers routed the line over the top of the dam to produce what is probably the most unusual "railway bridge" in Canada.*

53

Royal and Other Special Trains

LIKE ALL COMMONWEALTH COUNTRIES, Canada has provided rail transport for its royal visitors for more than a century. No special equipment is maintained for this purpose, but normal equipment is always prepared to meet the requirements of visiting members of the Royal House and for other visitors of special note. Throughout their century-and-a-quarter of service, Canada's railways have been called upon on many occasions to transport special loads or to perform special services. "Farmers' Specials" were used during the development of prairie lands to bring information on good agricultural methods. School cars, dentist's cars, doctor's cars and medical service cars are hauled on regular trains and left for a day or two on sidings near isolated small communities of railway workers.

54

54 *Canada's first royal railway service was provided for HRH Prince Edward of Wales in 1860 when he paid the first visit of any member of the royal family to Canada. Much of his travel in eastern Canada was on the early railways of the time, and this coach was specially constructed for his accommodation. Here at Saint John, New Brunswick, on the European and North American Railway, it is hauled by that small company's Locomotive No. 12, specially named* Prince of Wales.

55 *In great contrast is this view of TRH The Duke and Duchess of York (later to be King George V and Queen Mary) with members of their suite seated on the front of the locomotive of the Royal Train of the CPR at Glacier, British Columbia, prior to a short run through the beautiful scenery at this location during their visit to Canada in 1901.*

55

56 *To mark the centenary of the operation of the first railway train in Canada (see p. 8), Canadian National Railways built a replica of the* Dorchester, *the first locomotive to run in Canada on a public railway. Plans for the replica were prepared by members of the Canadian Railroad Historical Association. Placed on a special flat car, it was hauled at the* head of a special train by the latest CNR locomotive, a streamlined 4-8-4 No. 6400, along the CNR line to St. Jean which is almost identical with the original line of one hundred years before. Here No. 6400 is backing into Bonaventure Station, Montreal, to couple up with the special train.

56

57 *This is the Museum Train that was assembled by Canadian National Railways from existing old railway coaches and headed by two nineteenth-century steam locomotives. Staffed by enthusiastic guides, it toured Canada during 1956 and 1957, arousing much local interest at every stop.*

57

58 *The arrangements for the funeral of the Right Honourable W.L. Mackenzie King, for 24 years prime minister of Canada, were shared between Ottawa and Toronto. His body was conveyed from Ottawa to Toronto in a special train which carried also a large company of his government associates and friends. The special is here seen in Ottawa's former Union Station on 26 July 1950 with CNR 4-8-4 No. 6211 waiting for the arrival of the coffin, which was placed in the second of the two baggage cars.*

58

59 *This rare view from 1888 links the railway era with early Canada. A train of carts conveys furs valued at $75,000 from northern Hudson's Bay Company posts for shipment from Calgary to Montreal by the "new" railway which has replaced canoe transport. The water-portage system had been followed for the previous two hundred years.*

Unusual Loads and Functions

FEW COUNTRIES have such a major rail load as the wheat from the prairies which travels west to the port of Vancouver and east to Thunder Bay (p. 37) at the head of Lake Superior for trans-shipment to vessels which can sail down the St. Lawrence Seaway to the ocean. The main CPR line from Winnipeg to Thunder Bay is the second double-track line in Canada, doubled for handling this traffic. The Hudson Bay Railway, to the port of Churchill on Hudson Bay, was constructed essentially to give another ocean outlet for wheat. Wheat trains look much the same as other Canadian freight trains; special loads are more likely to catch the camera's attention. Here are a few examples of loads that betray their unusual character.

59

60 *It was just prior to the construction of railways in North America that the commercial slaughter of the buffalo on the Great Plains almost led to their extermination. Appropriately the new railways assisted in the rehabilitation of buffalo herds. This view shows the small herd of buffalo brought from Montana to Wainwright, Alberta, in 1909. In Canada's western National Parks the buffalo have prospered to such an extent that buffalo meat can now be occasionally purchased.*

60

61 *Christmas trees have gradually become traditional in North America, and the forests of Canada have long been an important source of the young tree harvest. This train was the first complete train load of Christmas trees to be shipped from Fredericton to Boston, Massachusetts. The date was 11 December 1905.*

61

62 *A number of railways have been built as private ventures purely for haulage of logs out of the forests, especially in British Columbia. Here is a Climax locomotive used on such a line of the Hillcrest Lumber Company. Built in 1912, it has been preserved in the Cowichan Valley Forest Museum at Duncan, B.C.*

63 *In eastern Canada there is still an active private logging railway, and it is within thirty miles of the capital city of Ottawa. This is the Thurso and Nation Valley Railway, built originally by the Singer Sewing Machine Company but now owned by the Thurso Pulp and Paper Company. This photograph from the days of steam operation shows the daily train bringing a full load of hardwood logs out of the forests north of the Ottawa River to the mill at Thurso.*

62

63

Steam at the Turn of the Century

BY THE FIRST DECADE of the twentieth century, the modern Canadian rail network was beginning to take form. There were to be amalgamations of companies, new lines to the west, great expansions of branch lines and improvement of facilities, but one could travel from coast to coast by rail, and in relative comfort—sleeping cars were in use, and the early parlour cars. Immigrants attracted to the opening west had to be content with much simpler accommodation. Motive power was naturally entirely provided by steam locomotives, which, while simple in design by comparison with those to be seen by mid-century, were reliable and economical in use. The main rail links with the United States had been established, so that rail travel throughout the continent was beginning to eliminate the isolation that characterized so many of the early settlements.

64 *A typical simple country station scene: Aultsville station in southern Ontario, with its small train headed by the Grand Trunk Railway Company's 2-6-0 No. 1008. Aultsville was one of the pleasant small towns which were flooded when the international dam and power house were built at Cornwall-Massena in association with the St. Lawrence Seaway, in the late fifties. While residents were relocated in a fine new town, the station building was fortunately preserved and moved to Upper Canada Village (a "folk village" in European style) where this local scene may still be enjoyed.*

64

65 *Naming of steam locomotives has not been as widely practised by Canadian railways as in Great Britain, but there have been some pleasant examples of this welcome feature. This photograph of the* Pontgravé *shows that the Dominion Atlantic Railway, a CPR subsidiary that serves the Bay of Fundy coast of Nova Scotia, named its maroon-coloured locomotives. The railway crest on the tender can also be seen; it includes a drawing of Evangeline, for the line runs through the "Land of Evangeline."*

65

66 *The Quebec and Lake St. John Railway, now part of Canadian National, also had named locomotives. The slightly barbaric decoration of the* Frank Ross's *headlight is at least a reminder that the railways of Canada pass through wild country for a considerable part of their total mileage. It is still possible to see wildlife in the forests from passing trains. Beaver dams still cause trouble with the flooding of some main lines. In more recent days, moose have been attracted onto rail lines by the "call" of the diesel locomotive.*

66

67 *Round House of the International Nickel Company of Canada Ltd. (now INCO), for their Sudbury operations, with their stud of yard locomotives neatly arranged; a view early in the century.*

67

68 *Railways were slowly spreading northwards. The Temiskaming and Northern Ontario Railway was an Ontario Government line, chartered in 1902, that was intended as a farm-development line but famous for leading (through its construction) to some of the remarkable mining developments of northern Ontario. This is the first train of the TNOR into Porcupine, one of the most famous of the gold mining "camps," on 1 July 1911.*

68

THE T&N.O. OFFICIAL TRAIN VISITS GOLDEN CITY, PORCUPINE, JULY 1/11. FIRST PASSENGER TRAIN IN THE GOLD CAMP

69 *Transcontinental rail travel was becoming known not only as a convenience but also as an attraction for both Canadians and visitors to Canada. Special observation cars were built to improve travellers' enjoyment of the spectacular scenery, on the CPR and on the new transcontinental lines as well. This view was taken on the Grand Trunk Pacific line at Moose Lake, Alberta, in the summer of 1915.*

69

70 *The first GTPR train from Winnipeg arrived in Prince Rupert (see p. 27) on 9 August 1914, and soon afterward regular passenger trains left this new west coast port for Winnipeg and eastern Canada. Later the GTPR used the National Transcontinental Railway east of Winnipeg that was completed in June 1915.*

71 *The first sleeping car on any railroad was probably designed in Hamilton, Ontario, by Samuel Sharp of the Great Western Railway in 1857. Models were made of this significant new piece of rolling stock and sent to Great Britain and France. This photograph is believed to show one of these models of Sharp's pioneer design.*

70

71

72 *The general appearance of more modern sleeping cars is now well known, if only because of their use in films, but in the early years of the century many newcomers to Canada travelled in much simpler versions known as Colonist Cars. Although the pictured passengers may not have been typical immigrants, this is a standard Colonist Car at the turn of the century, with utilitarian seats and somewhat primitive upper sleeping berths.*

72

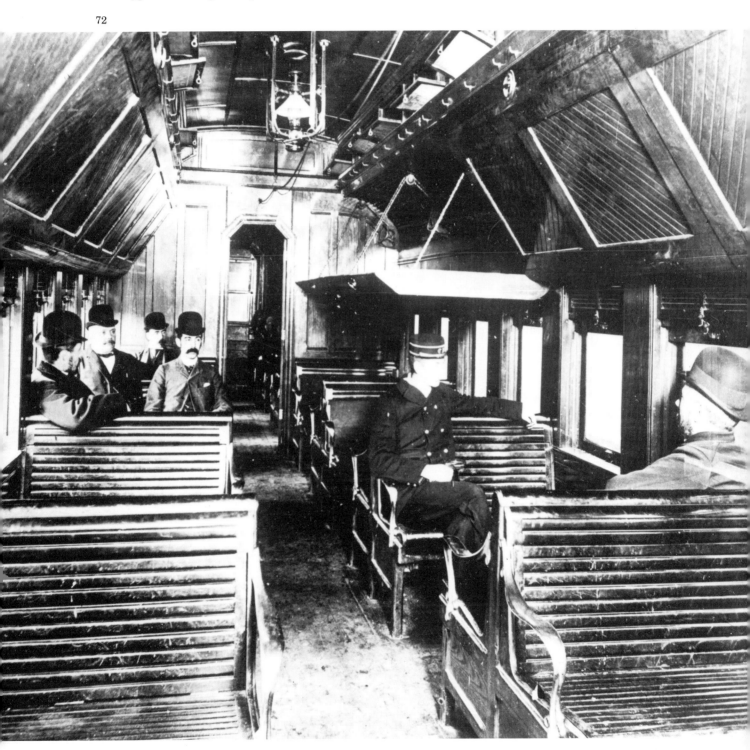

73 *For daytime travel, parlour cars came into wide use for those who could afford extra charges. This typical example of Victorian interior decoration calls for no comment beyond the fact that the photograph was taken in 1900 in one of the cars of the Canada Atlantic Railway which ran up the Ottawa Valley.*

73

Some Visitors

ONCE STANDARD GAUGE had been confirmed for Canadian railways (in 1870), with consequent abandonment of the "provincial gauge" of 5ft 6in, complete interchange with connecting lines from the United States of America became possible. There are now many direct connections, right across the continent, from St. Stephen on the Atlantic coast to White Rock on the Pacific coast, south of Vancouver. Freight cars of the continent can be seen on all Canadian main lines. The familiar emblems of CNR and CPR are to be seen, correspondingly, on lines all over the United States. Through passenger services to major cities of the United States had started by the turn of the century, from all the main cities of Canada. Some U.S. lines had running powers into Canadian terminals, as at Montreal. Some had their own short lines into Canada, as from Cornwall to Ottawa. Others used railways chartered by U.S. lines in Canada, such as the Michigan Central in southern Ontario which gave a short-cut between Detroit and Buffalo by running between Windsor and Niagara Falls. Both major Canadian railways developed subsidiary lines in the United States. Some attention to "visitors," in both directions, seems to be warranted even in so small a volume as this, if an overall view of the Canadian railway scene is to be presented.

74 *One of the main services between Montreal and New York was operated for many years (prior to the formation of AMTRAK in the United States) by the Delaware and Hudson Railroad in association with the New York Central, of which D.&H. is a subsidiary. Here is the day train from Montreal at its first suburban stop at Westmount in 1935. At its head is one of the D.&H. locomotives that were designed after the British style, in such contrast to the more usual North American style with all auxiliaries in full view. The daytime service was resumed in August 1974.*

74

75 *In the summer of 1933, a most welcome
visitor to Canada was the* Royal Scot *of the then*
London, Midland and Scottish Railway, *here
seen on display at Windsor Station (CPR)
in Montreal. This fine example of British
locomotive design ran on Canadian rails before
and after the U.S. part of its North American
tour, during which it ran over 11,000 miles and
was seen by over three million visitors.*

75

76 *One of the subsidiaries of Canadian National Railways in the United States is the Central Vermont Railroad (its name is accurately descriptive), control of which was acquired by the Grand Trunk Railway Company in 1899. Naturally dependent upon CNR for much of its engineering work, the Central Vermont had a fine stud of locomotives built in the U.S.A. This example was* photographed while at the Turcot (Montreal) locomotive depot of CNR.

77 *Another CNR subsidiary is the Grand Trunk Western Railroad, its name betraying its original acquisition by the Grand Trunk Railway Company. This is a GTWR Detroit-to-Muskegon train passing Bloomfield Hills, Michigan.*

76

77

Northern and Other Lines

THE FINE SERVICES of Canadian Pacific Rail and Canadian National Railways so dominate the Canadian railway scene that the equally good service of the score of other lines, though on a different scale, is all too easily forgotten. The unique White Pass line has already been mentioned (p. 26). The British Columbia (formerly Pacific Great Eastern) Railway is still expanding its scenic and busy network that serves the central and northern parts of its province. The Algoma Central (starting at Sault Ste. Marie) and Ontario Northland (formerly T&NO, see p.62) were pioneer northward lines in Ontario. Isolated lines on the north shore of the Gulf of St. Lawrence are now serving well the newly developed iron ore mines in that somewhat inhospitable region. And the Newfoundland Railway, after an independent (if somewhat harried) existence from 1882 to 1949, is now a part of Canadian National Railways. Its passenger service is now but a memory, but its narrow gauge freight service remains vital to the economy of the island which remembers being "the oldest Dominion."

78 *While other railways may be in decline, British Columbia Railway is very much in the ascendent. This provincially owned railway, running north from North Vancouver, increased its car loadings ten times in the twenty years between 1950 and 1970. Still expanding, its main-line system may soon be 1,800 miles long. Here is one of its southbound freight trains coming through the Cheakamus Canyon on its approach to Squamish at the head of Howe Sound.*

78

79 *A downbound freight passing through Whitehorse Station of the White Pass and Yukon Route on its 110-mile journey down to the sea at Skagway, Alaska. It has just left the large freight terminal which is now the centre of this railway's extensive trucking routes that fan out all over the Yukon mainly in service to the mines developed during the sixties. The gauge of this line is only three feet, but it provides full main-line service.*

80 *Bennett Station on the White Pass line, about halfway between Skagway and Whitehorse. Located at the head of Lake Bennett, this was the site of a bustling city of 10,000 in the days of the Klondike gold rush. Today the railway station, here seen with a summer-only daily passenger special, is the only inhabited building. In the foreground are steam locomotives and a rotary snowplough kept here on exhibition.*

79

80

81 *A mixed train of Northern Alberta Railways at Rycroft; the single passenger coach is at the rear end.*

82 *The* Newfie Bullet, *the narrow-gauge but fully equipped passenger train that crossed Newfoundland from Port-aux-Basques to St.*

John's. Here in the station at Cornerbrook, on the west coast, No. 321 is backing onto it to serve as pilot on the climb to the summit at Gaff Topsails. This bleak, windswept area is so exposed that trains had sometimes to be chained to the rails to avoid being blown off.

81

82

Railways and Cities

SO YOUNG A COUNTRY is Canada that some of its cities were founded because of early railways, with settlement springing up around locations selected "in the bush" as primitive divisional points. City expansion has surrounded railway lines so quickly, and passenger traffic in some cities has so declined (rather than expanded) that major relocation of railway lines has been called for in such centres as Ottawa and Saskatoon. Freight yards have been relocated away from cities, thus releasing valuable land for redevelopment. Suburban rail traffic is, at last, being rehabilitated, notably in Toronto with the aid of provincial funds but using the main (lakeshore) line of Canadian National Railways. Toronto and Montreal have new passenger subway systems; other cities are planning such rail services. Railways continue, therefore, to serve the cities of Canada well.

83 *Level crossings within cities are especially hazardous; they are gradually being eliminated. In the thirties a commonplace sight was a "post" signal box such as this one, which gave level crossing protection by lowering a simple barrier.*

84 *A steam suburban train in Montreal in the 1930s, on the CPR at Bordeaux to the north of the city. All too many of these local services have disappeared, but CPR still operates one well patronized service along the Lakeshore to the west of Montreal. It now has bi-level cars hauled by diesel locomotives.*

83

84

85 *Providing a contrast in railway terminals is this simple train shed of the Union Station in Saint John, New Brunswick. Served by CNR trains from Moncton, to the north, and CPR local services, this station was the departure point for well over half a century of the overnight CPR passenger train to Montreal that uses the "short line" through Maine.*

85

86 *This same train arrives in Montreal at the great Windsor Street Station, known throughout the century by travellers around the world. Here No. 2825, one of the CPR Royal Hudsons, is seen pulling out of Windsor Street, breasting the steep climb up to Westmount. The tower of the CPR office building is clearly visible in the background.*

86

87 *Canadian National Railways has, in the years since World War II, consolidated all its Montreal terminals in the convenient Central Station that now operates beneath a vast building and shopping complex. Lines leaving for the east, south and west are here seen emerging from the hidden station, with Montreal Harbour in the background.*

87

88 *Although not a main-line railway, the Toronto Transit Commission's subway system, the first in Canada, has made such a favourable impact upon the traffic pattern of this great city, now equal in size to Montreal, that this one view of a TTC train is warranted; it is emerging from the downtown tunnel section of the subway on its northbound run.*

88

89 *This could be one of several new freight marshalling yards, all equipped with modern automatic controls, that have replaced the old-style city freight yards. This fine example is CPR's Alyth Yard near Calgary, Alberta.*

89

90 *Canada is fortunate in having its full share of railway enthusiasts who have seen to it that examples of railway equipment now superseded have been preserved for public benefit. In most cities of Canada at least one splendid steam locomotive will be found, inactive and isolated but bearing mute testimony to the service that steam so long*

provided. Quite the most extensive collection of steam (and other) locomotives in Canada, and one of the best in North America, is that of the Canadian Railroad Historical Association. It is now housed at the Canadian Railway Museum at St-Constant to the south of Montreal, a mecca for all visitors with railway interest.

90

The Great Days of Steam

UNTIL THE END OF WORLD WAR II, all main-line Canadian railway service was provided by steam locomotives. Earlier in the century there had been some development of electric railways in some of the more populous parts of the country, reaching a peak about 1945, but these were always subsidiary to main-line services. Both main railways were experimenting with diesel haulage in 1949. Conversion on a large scale took place throughout the 1950s, with the result that steam haulage had all but disappeared by 1960. Despite all difficulties, the years of war showed the great potential of steam haulage when soundly designed, well maintained locomotives covered over 1,000 miles safely and regularly. There follows a small selection of the hundreds of views that could be used to illustrate this exciting chapter in the story of Canada's railways.

91 *Montreal-to-Toronto and Chicago afternoon train No. 15, the* International Limited, *passing Dixie, a Montreal suburb, at speed in the 1930s. The train was composed of both CPR and CNR rolling stock because pooling of the service was enforced by the effects of the great depression. Leaving from CPR's Windsor Station, these Canadian National-Canadian Pacific trains were hauled by fine-looking 4-6-4 locomotives designed by CNR for this service.*

91

92 *An unusual assembly of main-line Canadian National locomotives at the Turcot locomotive depot which serves Montreal.*

93 *In contrast, the single-stall locomotive shed at New Carlisle, Quebec, on the Gaspé branch-line serving the south shore of the lovely Gaspé Peninsula and connecting at Matapedia Junction with the main CNR line from Montreal to Halifax.*

92

93

94 *An eastbound CPR transcontinental train at White River, a divisional point for train servicing. It is reported to be the coldest place in eastern Canada. The photograph was taken when the air temperature was 20°F below zero.*

95 *A similar train leaving Calgary, Alberta, in summer with an old-type observation car at the right. Used for the daylight part of the journey through the mountains, the open-construction car gave splendid views such as are now obtained, in more comfort, from the modern dome cars.*

94

95

96 *One of the two 2-8-4s built by Montreal Locomotive Works Ltd., for the Toronto, Hamilton and Buffalo Railway, on a test run near Kinnear Station in 1928. The T.H.& B. line was jointly owned by CPR and the New York Central, providing a link between Hamilton and U.S. lines at Buffalo.*

Many pages could be filled with such standard views of locomotives as these, but the following examples must suffice, even though they show but three of many notable designs.

96

97 *T&NOR No. 1103 at North Bay in 1941; one of four machines built by the Canadian Locomotive Company in 1936 and 1937, mainly for hauling* The Northland. *The name of this daily train was carried on the running board skirt when the engine was used for this service.*

98 *The only really controversial locomotive design in Canada in recent years was the F-1 class of CPR, No. 2912 of which is seen here at Winnipeg in 1947. Some thought them to be* elegant machines; some did not. They gave good service after their introduction in 1937, on light passenger trains.

99 *The heaviest locomotives ever constructed in Canada were the Selkirks of CPR, designed for operation over the steep grades in the mountains, especially between Revelstoke and Calgary. Thirty-six of these fine machines were built between 1938 and 1949; here is one of the second batch at Banff in 1939.*

97

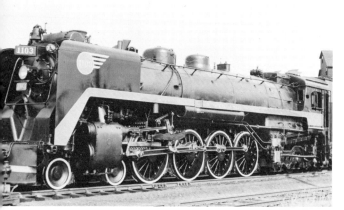

98

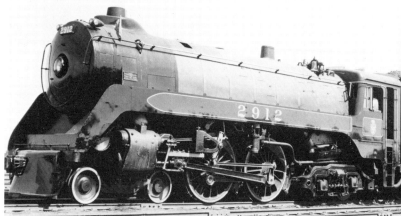

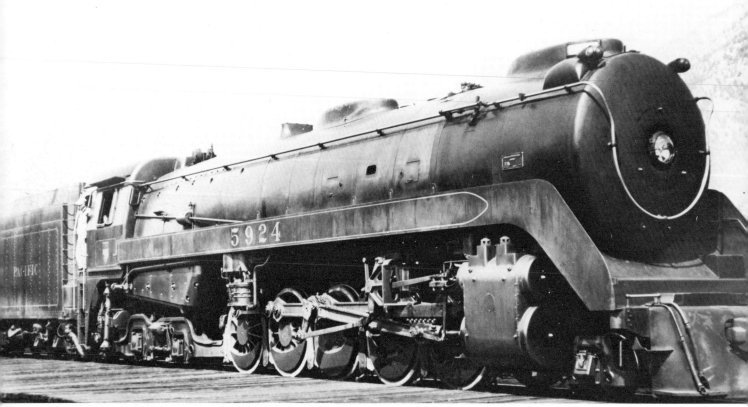

99

100 *One of the later Selkirks on an acceptance-test run on freight service, returning to Montreal from Smith's Falls. Four days after this view was taken, on 12 March 1949, CPR took delivery of its last steam locomotive, No. 5935 of the same class.*

100

101 *In its early years, after introduction by the newly formed Canadian National Railways, the Continental Limited transcontinental train travelled from North Bay to Cochrane over the lines of the T&NOR in order to get on to the main east-west line of the (old) National Transcontinental Railway, part of the new CNR. This 1929 view shows the northbound train, hauled by a T&NOR locomotive, in Cobalt Station, very close to where the original find of silver ore was made during the construction of this line.*

101

102 *Branch lines came and went in the busy days of steam. Here is the once-weekly mixed train run on the Silver Centre branch of the T&NOR to serve an important construction job for which all the supplies came in by rail. With mining at Silver Centre decreasing, the branch was abandoned soon after the construction work finished.*

103 *With only one train a week, and the nearest road five miles away, access to the job noted in 102 was difficult; hence occasional unauthorized but helpful use of the section man's speeder for emergency journeys.*

103

102

104 *There were small branch lines down by the sea also, this being mixed train No. 3 of the Cumberland Railway and Coal Co. Ltd., from East Southampton and Parrsboro to Springhill Junction,*

104

105 *Divisional points were busy places when main line trains came through and passengers took exercise on the platforms while locomotive and train were being serviced. Here is a typical stop, at Chapleau in northern Ontario on the main line of the CPR, with a westbound transcontinental train in the station. The local locomotive shed can be seen in the background, and the associated freight yard.*

105

106 *As part of the keen competition between CNR and CPR in the late twenties, a high point in luxury travel was reached in 1929 when parlour cars on Canadian National trains were equipped for radio reception while travelling; passengers could listen through headphone sets. With the advent of the great depression later that year, the practice did not long continue.*

106

107 *As an epilogue to this glance at the trains that have gone, here is a view of an eastbound Canadian Pacific passenger train climbing the steep grade out of Field, B.C., through one of the spiral tunnels built to ease the overall grade. The train engine is one of the Selkirks, piloted by No. 5809, a 2-10-2. The last coach of the train (just entering the tunnel) is one of the special mountain observation cars.*

107

Railways of Today

THE RAILWAYS OF CANADA continue to serve the country well. All services are now diesel-hauled, but so great has been the increase in freight tonnage, especially of coal from the mines of Alberta and British Columbia through the mountains to ocean shipping points, that serious study is being given to the electrification of critical sections of main line. As is the case throughout North America, airlines and the automobile have made serious inroads into rail passenger traffic, but Canadian National still maintains excellent main-line services such as those from Halifax to Montreal and from Montreal to Toronto. Both main railways continue to operate their transcontinental trains. These are crowded in summer months but not well patronized in winter, so that the future of this world-famous service rests in the hands of the Canadian Transport Commission which exercises regulatory control over all rail services. Apart from this one uncertainty, the future of Canada's railways is assured.

108 *An interesting example of far-sighted development was the experimentation with diesel haulage on Canadian National Railways in the late twenties. Under the dynamic leadership of Sir Henry Thornton, this "largest railway system in North America" had to be welded into an integrated entity from the many lines brought together under its aegis. A diesel-driven railcar was operated from coast to coast without its engine stopping. Here is the experimental diesel locomotive then constructed passing Dixie station, near Montreal. The experiments did not continue, but they pointed the way to developments of just twenty years later.*

108

109 *On 24 April 1955 both Canadian main railways introduced entirely new schedules with cuts averaging fifteen hours off previous transcontinental running times. This was the first beneficial result of diesel haulage. CPR also introduced an entirely new suite of stainless steel streamlined trains for the cross-country service, dome cars being included for the first time. Here is the initial western run of* The Canadian *(as the new CPR train was called) on that memorable day, leaving Ottawa's (old) Union station. The East Block of Canada's Parliament Buildings is on the right, the CNR Chateau Laurier hotel on the left, and in the centre the entrance locks of the 140-year old Rideau Canal to Kingston.*

109

110 *Craigellachie! The cairn with its plaque marks the location of the driving of the last spike of the CPR in November 1885. A modern diesel-hauled way-freight passes on its way to Revelstoke, British Columbia.*

111 *Eastbound transcontinental train ready to leave Prince Rupert, now a fine small modern city and active port in contrast with its pioneer character when the view on p. 63 was taken. Joining the* Supercontinental *from Vancouver at Jasper, the through coaches on this train will travel 3,106 miles to Montreal.*

110

111

112 *The CNR* Supercontinental *at Punnichy, Saskatchewan. The grain elevators are typical of all such stations on the prairies; the riders add a somewhat unusual local touch.*

113 *The CPR* Canadian *on its westbound run during the brief stop at Sicamous, a pleasantly located lake-side station.*

112

113

114 *Typical of modern Canadian main-line diesel-hauled trains is the* Rapido *service, one of the fine sets of trains with which Canadian National Railways maintains its Montreal-Toronto daily service. This train, here seen at its brief service stop at Brockville, does the 335-mile trip, with two suburban stops, in one minute under five hours.*

114

115 *Modern local services and branch line trains are now provided by means of single or multiple rail-diesel-cars (RDCs) such as this CPR car, here seen at the disused engine shed at Maniwaki, the terminal of an attractive branch-line running north from Ottawa up the Gatineau River valley.*

115

116 *The CNR* Supercontinental *at Windy Point, Jasper National Park, Jasper, Alberta.*

117 *The CPR* Canadian *at Ottertail Creek, east of Field, British Columbia.*

116

117

118 *The end of steel! The two tank cars occupy the last few feet of a siding which forms the northern end of the Great Slave Lake Railway. This point is one mile beyond the main freight yard of this new line at Hay River on the shore of Great Slave Lake, Northwest Territories, north of the 60° parallel. Direct rail connection exists between this far-northern point and all the rail lines of Canada and the United States.*

118